IN

HER MOTHER'S

Footsteps

GWEN GRAFFENREED

To order additional copies of this book, contact:
Xlibris
1-800-455-039
www.xlibris.com.au
Orders@Xlibris.com.au

ISBN: Softcover   978-1-4628-8302-8
         EBook   978-1-9845-8725-1

Print information available on the last page

Rev. date: 06/27/2020

Dedication

To my mother Rebecca, my grandmothers, aunts, and other family members who influenced my life by instilling in me strong family ties, love, and cultural pride.

To Sacred Heart Roman Catholic Church, Greenville, Mississippi; Mt. Horeb Missionary Baptist Church, Greenville, Mississippi; St. Barbara Catholic Church, St. Louis, Missouri; St. Patrick Catholic Church, St. Louis, Missouri; Our Lady of Peace Catholic Church, Cleveland, Ohio; Lane Metropolitan CME Church, Cleveland, Ohio; and the National Mental Health Organization.

Acknowledgments

Special thanks to my sister Geraldine for her encouragement and support.

To Sandra Beane Milton, Anita Eddie, Barbara McIntyre, Jannie Hayes, Charlotte McIntyre, Jocelyn Winn, Ramona Menefee, Nina Dailey, Dolores Thompson, Elaine Whitlock, Bertha Venson, and Theresa Palmer.

To the African American Genealogical Society of Cleveland, Ohio.

References:

Beacon Lights of the Race, Encyclopedia
and Census Tracts

During a family visit to my mother's hometown Greenville, Mississippi, I remember the many conversations about family members. Family stories my family shared with us sitting on porch in Greenville, Mississippi, about my maternal great-grandmother. My great-grandmother was one of the family's early women pioneers. She was born Rebecca Covington, around 1877, in Greenville, Mississippi. She was the daughter of Mellissa Tiggles and R. A. Covington. My great-grandparents were born in Virginia around 1850s and migrated to Louisiana around 1875 then Greenville, Mississippi, in early 1877.

During 1877–1900, it was known as the Gilded Age in the state of Mississippi. It was a time of steady economics and social progress due to the opportunities. African Americans began acquiring land ownership during 1870s and 1880s. The family was fortunate to obtain land from hard work and steady employment. During that time, men were breadwinners for the family, and some of the women began to venture out.

Great-grandmother was a teacher; she had a love for books. She was very active in her community and had strong kinship bonds. Family time was when women worked in the kitchen together, preparing dinner, eating dinner with tablecloth on the table, sitting on the porch or in the yard, reading books, hand sewing, writing letters, and having conversations with family as well with neighbors. Gardening was one of many families' outdoor activities and food for the family. People were very respectful in the family; they would write letters as well as send pecans, quilts, cakes, clothes, cards, and shoes to loved ones. Writing was a way families communicated during those times. Reading and writing was considered a gift. Writing was so personal, and it taught you how to be patient.

She married into the Reed family and became a professional teacher, and Great-grandfather Burl was a drayman, and both were employed by the city of Greenville, Mississippi. Great-grandfather and other family members were instrumental in steering her toward a teaching career. The family was always encouraged to have a love for books. During the early years, so many people were deprived of reading or having books. Books became a family treasure. It continues to be in our family today.

She was very involved in her community, like so many people during that time. She lived around multicultural families. Some were teachers, draymen, farmers, seamstresses, homemakers, barbers, carpenters, bricklayers, nursemaids, and physicians.

One of her well-known neighbors was E. P. Brown, the community physician. He was born in Holmesville, Pike County, Mississippi, in 1856. He held many careers during his life. He was a teacher and schoolmaster at an early age. He decided to change his profession and attend Meharry Medical College and graduated in 1886. He was one of the respected Negro physicians during his time. Dr. Brown moved to Greenville, Mississippi, around 1889 for more challenges. In Greenville, Mississippi, it was a larger town and more opportunities. He was one of the wealthiest Negroes in the state of Mississippi during his time. He became one of the presidents of Delta Penny Savings Bank run by Negroes of Greenville, Mississippi, organized in 1907 and incorporated in 1908. Another president banker that is documented was J. W. Strauther, who was well-known businessman in his own right. He was born in 1867 and was a hard worker and was not afraid of work. He was educated and owned many businesses in Greenville. He had a draying and transportation business and employed many men in the community.

In the early days, people were very neighborly.

J. W. Strauther was an undertaker in Greenville as well as property owner. His professions included bricklayer, porter, delivery driver, supreme vice chancellor of the Knights of Pythias, and head of the women's department of Supreme Lodge of Knights of Pythias of the World, supreme treasurer of the Knights and Daughters of Temple of America, manager of the Blade Publishing, member in the Board of Deacons at Mt. Horeb Missionary Baptist Church in Greenville, Mississippi.

Great-grandmother Rebecca was engaged in her community. She became a mother of four children during 1901–1915. Times were challenging, but family was important. A sense of family pride is more valuable than dollars and cents. Family members were there to support one another. She was engaged in her community; her mother was a seamstress and sewed clothes for a living, and her brother was a carpenter and helped build homes in the community in early 1900s.

Many women in the family were active in the community. Great-grandma Rebecca, as well as my great-great-aunt Annie, exhibited the strengths of multicultural families throughout the years—strong kinship bonds, adaptability in family roles, strong work ethics, strong religious beliefs, and strong emphasis on education achievement. Family members were engaged in early settlement of Greenville Community by holding position with the city. They shared and worked together to make it better for many people to live in harmony.

During the early days, Mississippi was a very challenging state to live in as well as the city of Greenville. Just reading the history of the state of Mississippi was something to imagine. People of many cultures were poor and struggling to survive. Some did survive by the assistance of Europeans, Jewish, Native Americans, Italians, African Americans, and Asians.

The professions of women in the family in the early days were homemakers, seamstress, gardeners, teachers, housemaids, cooks nursemaids, receptionist, and secretaries. Women were taught a sense of family pride. They were devoted to the family, cultural, and civic activities in the community. Women were taught to be women and take care of themselves and their families.

Great-great-grandmother Covington was a professional seamstress, and Grandmother Lee worked at Colored King's Daughters Home in Greenville, Mississippi. Grandmother Lee was an awesome cook, and she collected and saved almost everything. One treasure she began was hand sewing a quilt by using old material from family members' clothing. It is very sentimental to the family because she started making the quilt in Greenville, Mississippi, in 1940s and brought it to Cleveland, Ohio, in the early 1960s and kept adding old family clothing. The hand stitching is just awesome, and it remains in excellent condition. She taught women in the family how to have patience by watching her sew and taking pride in what you do. The material pieces remind me of my family and the families' good times and their times of struggle.

Great-grandmother Rebecca and Great-grandfather Burl passed away at early ages. Great-great-aunt Annie undertook the awesome responsibility of mothering their four children. She raised her niece and nephews quite well. They became productive members of the community. They owned property on the South 69 feet of North 138 feet, Lot 2, Block 1 of the O. M. Blanton Addition to the said city of Greenville, Mississippi. Some of the family worshiped at Historic Sacred Heart Roman Catholic Church and Mt. Horeb Missionary Baptist Church in Greenville.

FOR AND IN CONSIDERATION of $1.00 cash to me in hand paid, the receipt of which is hereby acknowledged, I, ██████ ██████, hereby quitclaim and convey unto WILL REED all of my interest in the following described property in the City of Greenville, County of Washington, State of Mississippi, to-wit:

The north 69 feet of Lot 2 of Block 1 of the O. M. Blanton Addition to the said City.

This conveyance is intended to do away with the provision in the deed from me to Will Reed conveying the said property, dated March 14, 1952, to the effect that I should receive one-half of any sum over and above $3500.00 received by the said Will Reed for the said property in the event he sold the same.

This deed is intended to convey any interest I may now have in the said property so that the said Will Reed may sell and dispose of the same if he wishes to do so, free from any obligation on his part to pay to me any sum of money.

WITNESS my signature, this the 28th day of July,

---

hereby acknowledged, I, ██████████, a single man and the only child and sole heir-at-law of Annie L. ██████ a widow, who died intestate on March 10, 1952, do hereby sell, convey and warrant unto Will Reed an undivided one-half interest in the following described real property situated in the City of Greenville, County of Washington, State of Mississippi, to-wit:

The South 69 feet of the North 138 feet of Lot 2 of Block 1 of the O. M. Blanton Addition to the said City of Greenville.

This conveyance is made subject to an outstanding life interest in Annie Pope as reserved by her in that certain deed dated June 21, 1948, and recorded in Book 378, at page 66 of the Land Records of said County. However, all right, title and interest acquired by Annie L. Howard by virtue of said conveyance aforesaid is hereby conveyed unto the grantee herein.

WITNESS my signature this 14th day of March, 1952.

STATE OF MISSISSIPPI
COUNTY OF WASHINGTON

Personally appeared before me, the undersigned Notary Public in and for the aforesaid state and county, the within named PETER HOWARD, who acknowledged that he signed and delivered the foregoing instrument as his own act and deed on the day and year therein mentioned.

Given under my hand and official seal this 14th day of March, 1952.

Joan A. Pont
Notary Public

My commission expires December 28, 1955.

Many of the family began to move north around the 1940s. They mastered to survive the great 1927 Mississippi floods because they knew what hardships and sacrifices are about. Many of the family moved to St. Louis, Missouri, Detroit, Cincinnati, Chicago, and Cleveland. The family moved slowly by obtaining housing and employment; then they would send for family members to join and help them to obtain housing and employment.

My paternal grandparents moved to Cleveland, Ohio, around the 1930s and brought property from an Italian family and an Irish family in the Woodland neighborhood. They lived in a diverse neighborhood with African Americans, Italians, Russians, Jewish and Europeans. Granddaddy worked for the Cleveland Illuminating Company for some thirty-six years. He started out as a laborer and then was promoted to a group leader and supervised fourteen men until his retirement. He had strong work ethics and was well respected by his colleagues. My father worked for the Illuminating Company as a cable splicer as well, and Uncle "Spud" Leroy was a professional ball player for the Vikings.

Women Who Shaped the Characters of Our Family

Maternal great-grandmother Rebecca was the mother of four children—Burl, Annie Lee, Lucious, and Will. She and Grandfather Burl died at early ages, and Great-great-aunt Annie undertook the awesome responsibility of mothering their children.

BELL, Photographer,

Greenville, Miss.

Died in 1917 and the photograph survived
the flood of Mississippi in 1927.

Maternal great-grandmother Mamie was a true Irish women who believed in strong kinship bonds.

Great-great-aunt Annie instilled cultural pride through family photographs, lithographs, strengths, values, and a sense of family pride, which are all more valuable than dollars and cents.

Lithograph of Negro bankers and cashiers of Mississippi dated 1909, survived the 1927 Mississippi floods.

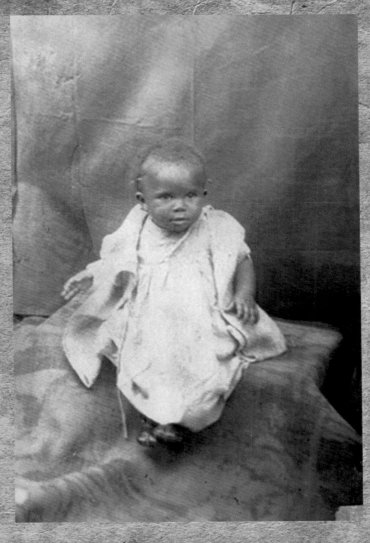

Photograph of my mother, Rebecca, 1925.
She survived the 1927 Mississippi floods.

My mother, Rebecca, was a homemaker and attended Historical Sacred Heart Catholic School in Greenville, Mississippi. The church is well-known for educating African American youth. She taught me to be caring and conscientious and the importance of being independent.

Photograph of my mother, Rebecca.

Grandma Caroline taught my sister and me how to hand sew dolls as well as make dolls out of brown paper bags. She made dolls for us and put a lot of time, love, and creativity into the dolls that she made. She also made little quilts for our dolls by hand. I believe these seeds sown by my mother and grandmothers sparked the interest I developed for collecting dolls and creating dolls of my own. She gave my sister Geraldine and me cooking lessons. We learned cooking from scratch and the importance of it, taking care of self, the family treasures, and photographs. Grandmother Caroline worked at Colored King's Daughters Home in Greenville, Mississippi.

Grandma Caroline at a very young age

A 1950 gold toned bowl

1940 sewing notion can

Paternal grandma Maggie was a serious and very business-type person. She kept the family close together and taught the family to be proud of our Irish heritage. She was the gem of the family and a friend to the end. Grandma Maggie was a homemaker.

Aunt Katherine dressed nice and I watched how she dressed, and I learn the importance of being a lady. She was an awesome seamstress and was well respected. Aunt Katherine and Uncle Frank managed a movie theater in Cleveland, Ohio, in the 1960s.

Great Aunt Katie was quiet and kept the family together as family members departed this life. She was such a remarkable person. I spent many weekends with her. I remember how she made the biggest pancakes, and I enjoyed them. Aunt Katie was a homemaker.

Aunt Katie, in the middle, and her brothers—Great Uncles Bill and Charlie.

Aunt Arnetta was a graduate of Central High School and was active in Lane Metropolitan CME Church in Cleveland, Ohio. She moved to California in 1954 and worked as a dental assistant. Then she decided to establish her own record and music business. Later, she decided to accept a permanent employment with Broadway Stores as top salesperson and stock consultant.

Women in my family have shaped my character in many ways. I am proud my family cared enough to teach me the skills I needed to survive in this world. According to Strengthsfinders 2.0 Assessment, my top five strengths are relator, learner, input, strategic, and achiever.

My cousin Dolores

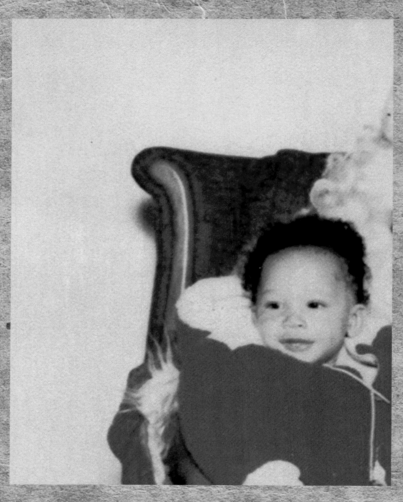

My beloved son, Jason at seven months old

Myself, cousin Nina and Earl Dailey

My wonderful sister Geraldine

Printed in the United States
By Bookmasters